# Rooted &
# RISING

21 Devotional Companions for
Strength in Every Season

## Dr. Larry L. Charles II

Author: Dr. Larry L. Charles II
Publisher: Kingdom News Publication Services, LLC.

Printed in the United States of America.
ISBN 978-1-955127-43-1

✦ ◆ ✦

A Scripture-based devotional for those
navigating illness, transition, grief, or quiet
struggle—featuring 21 companions of grace,
truth and spiritual resilience.

✦ ◆ ✦

The tree on the cover of this devotional
is intentional. Life is layered; on the
surface, we show up smiling, serving,
and surviving—but that is only part of
the story. Beneath the surface, roots
stretch through grief, illness, transition,
and quiet struggle. They twist through
questions we haven't voiced, wounds
we haven't named, and prayers we're
still learning to pray. This devotional
was written for that hidden place.

✦ ◆ ✦

# Table of Contents

✦✦✦

# Table of Contents

# Introduction
# How to Use This Book

This devotional is not meant to be rushed. It's a companion for the slow days, the heavy seasons and the quiet moments when you need to remember you're not alone. Each entry introduces a personified companion—such as Hope, Grace, or Resilience—rooted in Scripture and designed to walk with you through whatever you're facing.

You can read one entry per day, per week, or whenever you need a word of presence. Each devotional includes:

- A brief reflection to center your heart
- A Scripture to anchor your spirit
- A micro-practice to embody the truth
- A daily decision to move forward with intention
- Thoughts For Today—a place to journal your thoughts

Whether you're navigating physical illness, emotional fatigue, spiritual dryness, or relational strain, these companions are here to remind you: you are held, you are known, and you are rising, rooted in Christ.

# *Broken*
## THE SACRED CRACKS

✦✦✦

## When Brokenness Shows Up

Brokenness doesn't demand explanation. It arrives in the quiet collapse of what once held together. When brokenness shows up, it invites surrender, not defeat, and opens the door to divine restoration.

## Devotional Reflection

In the Chrisitan story, brokenness is not the end; it's the beginning of redemption. Scripture is filled with cracked vessels, wounded prophets, and weary disciples who meet God not in their strength, but in their surrender. The cross itself is the ultimate symbol of brokenness embraced and transformed.

When we allow brokenness to speak, we stop hiding and start

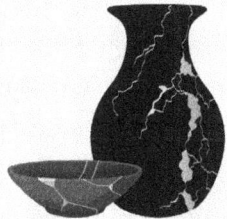

healing. We become like clay in the Potter's hand; malleable, honest, ready to be reshaped. The world may see weakness, but heaven sees readiness.

The Japanese have an art form called Kintsugi that takes broken pottery and repairs it with gold and other precious metals. Where we throw things that are broken away, they don't. They take it and restore it, and they don't hide the cracks. They highlight the cracks by putting light in the vessel so that they now share their testimony, and with the gold in the cracks the vessel is more valuable after the break than before the break.

God is not repelled by breaks. He is near the brokenhearted. And in those sacred cracks, His light shines through.

## Scripture Reference

*The Lord is near to the brokenhearted and saves the crushed in spirit.*
**Psalm 34:18 KJV**

## Micro-Practice

Sit quietly with God for five minutes today. No words. Just presence. Let Him fill the cracks.

## Daily Decision

Choose to name one area of brokenness in prayer—not to fix it, but to offer it unto God.

# Today's Thoughts

# *Hope*
## THE QUIET COMPANION

✦◆✦

## When Hope Shows Up

Hope doesn't shout; it whispers. It doesn't erase fear; it stands beside it. When hope shows up, it reminds you that God's promises are still unfolding, even in the waiting.

## Devotional Reflection

Hope is not wishful thinking; it is anchored trust in God's character. In seasons when outcomes are uncertain and strength feels thin; hope reminds us that God is not finished. Scripture tells us that hope does not disappoint, because God's love has been poured into our hearts (Romans 5:5). This is not a fragile optimism; it's a Spirit-born assurance.

Hope shows up in the sunrise, in the kindness of a stranger, in the quiet moment when you remember a verse that once carried you. It's the belief that even here, God is working. Even now, he is near. Hope doesn't deny the storm; it holds fast through it, tethered to the one who calms it.

## Scripture Reference

*We have this hope as an anchor
for the soul, firm and secure.*
**Hebrews 6:19 NIV**

## Micro-Practice

Speak one promise of God aloud today. Let it settle into your spirit.

## Daily Decision

Choose to expect God's presence today, even if you don't yet see the outcome.

# Today's Thoughts

_____

_____

_____

_____

_____

_____

_____

_____

_____

_____

_____

_____

_____

_____

_____

_____

# *Rise*
## THE REBEL SOUL

✦✦✦

## When Rise Shows Up

Rise doesn't wait for strength; it responds to grace. It doesn't erase the fall; it honors the getting up. When Rise shows up, it reminds you that resurrection is always possible.

## Devotional Reflection

The Christian life is marked by resurrection—not just once, but daily. Rise is the companion who echoes the empty tomb, reminding you that defeat is never final. Whether you're recovering from treatment, facing discouragement, or simply weary, Rise says, "Get up!"

Jesus met the paralyzed, the grieving, the

ashamed and said, "Rise." Not because they were ready, but because He was present. Rise is not about performance; it is about participation in God's redemptive movement. Every time you choose to keep going, you reflect the risen Christ. And that is holy ground.

## Scripture Reference

*Arise, shine, for your light has come, and the glory of the Lord rises upon you.*
**Isaiah 60:1 NIV**

## Micro-Practice

Stand up slowly today and say aloud, "I rise in grace today."

## Daily Decision

Take one step toward something life-giving. Call someone, pray, walk or rest with intention.

# Today's Thoughts

_____

_____

_____

_____

_____

_____

_____

_____

_____

_____

_____

_____

_____

_____

_____

_____

_____

_____

_____

# *Peace*
## THE STEADY HEALER

✦✦✦

## When Peace Shows Up

Peace doesn't silence the storm; it speaks in the storm. It doesn't demand calm; it offers it. When peace shows up, it reminds you that Jesus still says, "Peace, be still."

## Devotional Reflection

Peace is not the absence of trouble; it is the presence of Christ. In John 14:27, Jesus says, "My peace I give you... Not as the world gives." This peace is deeper than circumstances. It's the steady healer that calms your breath, quiets your mind, and anchors your soul.

In the middle of diagnosis, surgery or grief, peace may feel elusive. But it's not gone; it's waiting to be received. Peace is the Spirit's gift, not your achievement. It's the stillness that comes when you remember who holds you. And when you welcome peace, you begin to heal from the inside out.

## Scripture Reference

*You will keep in perfect peace those whose minds are steadfast, because they trust in you.*
**Isaiah 26:3 NIV**

## Micro-Practice

Pause for one minute today. Breathe deeply. Whisper, "Jesus, be my peace."

## Daily Decision

Choose to trust God with one thing that feels out of control.

# Today's Thoughts

# Grace

## THE QUIET GENEROSITY

✦✦✦

### When Grace Shows Up

Grace doesn't wait for worthiness; it arrives carrying mercy. It doesn't tally mistakes; it offers restoration. When Grace shows up, it reminds you that love is a gift and not a transaction.

### Devotional Reflection

Grace is the heartbeat of the gospel. It's the unearned favor of God, poured out in Christ. In seasons of suffering or when you feel weak, unproductive, or ashamed, Grace says, "You are still loved."

Paul reminds us that God's power is made perfect in weakness (2 Corinthians 12:9). Grace doesn't ignore your struggle; it meets you there.

This companion shows up in the forgiveness you didn't expect, the kindness you didn't earn, and the strength you didn't summon. Grace is the reminder that you don't have to be enough, because Jesus already is. And when you receive Grace, you begin to live from abundance, not scarcity.

## Scripture Reference

*For from his fullness we have all received, grace upon grace.*
**John 1:16 ESV**

## Micro-Practice

Speak this aloud: I receive grace today not because I've earned it, but because it's mine in Christ.

## Daily Decision

Let go of one self-judgment. Replace it with a truth from Scripture.

# Today's Thoughts

# Steady
## The Unshaken Presence

✦✦✦

## When Steady Shows Up

Steady doesn't rush or retreat. It stays. When Steady shows up, it reminds you that God's faithfulness is not seasonal; it's eternal.

## Devotional Reflection

In the shifting terrain of life, Steady is the presence that holds. It's the rhythm of Scripture, the constancy of prayer, the friend who keeps showing up. God's character is described as a rock, a refuge, a stronghold, and Steady reflects that truth. You don't have to be unshaken to be held by what is.

Psalm 62 reminds us: "He alone is my rock

and my salvation, my fortress; I shall not be shaken." Steady is not about perfection; it is about presence. It's the grace that meets you every morning, the Spirit that intercedes when you can't find words. When you welcome Steady, you begin to trust that God is not moved by your weakness; He is moved by love.

## Scripture Reference

*He alone is my rock and my salvation, my fortress: I shall not be shaken.*
**Psalm 62:6 ESV**

## Micro-Practice

Return to one spiritual rhythm today: Scripture, prayer, or silence. Let it steady you.

## Daily Decision

Choose to trust God with one thing that feels unstable.

# Today's Thoughts

# *Light*
## THE REVEALER AND GUIDE

✦✦✦

## When Light Shows Up

Light doesn't erase darkness; it reveals truth within it. When light shows up, it reminds you that God is still guiding, even when the path is unclear.

## Devotional Reflection

Light is one of the most powerful metaphors in Scripture. Jesus says, "I am the light of the world," (John 8:12), and His presence illuminates even the darkest places. Wherever you find yourself today, light may feel dim, but it is never absent. It shows up in clarity, in kindness, in the Word that speaks directly to your soul.

Light doesn't always change your

circumstances; it changes your vision. It helps you see what's still beautiful, what's still true, what's still possible. Psalm 119 says, "Your word is a lamp unto my feet and a light unto my path." When you welcome Light, you begin to walk not by sight, but by faith.

## Scripture Reference
*The light shines in the darkness, and the darkness has not overcome it.*
**John 1:5 NIV**

## Micro-Practice
Read one verse slowly today. Let it be your light.

## Daily Decision
Choose to notice one beautiful thing God is revealing even in this season.

# Today's Thoughts

# Tender
## THE COURAGE OF GREATNESS

✦◆✦

## When Tender Shows Up

Tender doesn't fix; it abides. When Tender shows up, it reminds you that gentleness is a form of holy strength.

## Devotional Reflection

Jesus was tender with the broken, the grieving, the ashamed. He didn't rush their healing; He honored their humanity. In Matthew 11, He says, "I am gentle and humble in heart, and you will find rest for your souls." Tender is the companion who reflects that posture.

In life's difficulties, tenderness may feel rare, but it is powerful. It's the friend who listens without judgement or advice, the Spirit who groans on your behalf. Tenderness is not weakness—it's the courage to be soft in a hard world. When you welcome Tender, you begin to heal in ways force never could.

## Scripture Reference

*Let your gentleness be evident*
*to all. The Lord is near.*
**Philippians 4:5 NIV**

## Micro-Practice

Speak gently to yourself today. Let your words reflect Christ's tenderness.

## Daily Decision

Offer one act of gentleness to yourself or someone else.

# Today's Thoughts

# Enough

## THE DEFENDER OF IDENTITY

✦✦✦

## When Enough Shows Up

Enough doesn't compare or compete. It shows up and says, "You are already loved." When Enough shows up, it reminds you that your worth is secure in Christ.

## Devotional Reflection

In the season of suffering, it's easy to feel like you're not enough; too weak, too tired, too behind. But the gospel says otherwise. You are chosen, beloved, redeemed not because of what you do, but because of who God is. Ephesians 2:8 reminds us, "It is by grace you

have been saved, through faith and this is not of yourselves."

Enough is the companion who silences shame. It's the truth that your identity is not diminished by your difficulty. You are not less. You are not forgotten. You are enough because Christ is. When you welcome Enough, you begin to live from grace, not striving.

## Scripture Reference
*My grace is sufficient for you, for my power is made perfect in weakness.*
**2 Corinthians 12:9 NIV**

## Micro-Practice
Write down one truth about who you are in Christ. Read it aloud.

## Daily Decision
Let go of one lie about your worth. Replace it with Scripture.

# Today's Thoughts

# Rooted

## THE KEEPER OF DEEP STRENGTH

✦◆✦

## When Rooted Shows Up

Rooted doesn't resist the storm—it prepares for it. When rooted shows up, it reminds you that strength grows in hidden places.

## Devotional Reflection

Rooted is the companion who anchors you in truth. Psalm one describes the one who meditates in the word day and night shall be like a tree planted by the rivers of water that bring forth fruit in their season and their

leaves shall not wither and whatsoever they do it shall prosper. Rooted reminds you of what hasn't changed: God's character, His promises, nor His presence.

This companion draws strength from Scripture, from prayer, from memory. It's the part of you that remembers who you are, even when everything else shifts. Rooted doesn't prevent the storm; it helps you stand through it. And when you welcome Rooted, you begin to trust that healing is not just forward; it's downward. It's depth. It's staying.

## Scripture Reference
*They will be like a tree planted by the water... It does not fear when heat comes: its leaves are always green.*
**Jeremiah 17:8 NIV**

## Micro-Practice
Return to one Scripture that has grounded you. Sit with it today.

## Daily Decision
Choose one truth to hold onto; no matter what changes.

# Today's Thoughts

# *Restore*
## THE WEAVER OF WHOLENESS

✦✦✦

## When Restore Shows Up

Restore doesn't rush. It gathers what's been scattered and begins to mend. When restore shows up, it reminds you that healing is not about returning; it's about becoming.

## Devotional Reflection

Life can unravel in many ways through loss, burnout, betrayal, or transition. Restore is the companion who enters the fray with the needle of grace and the thread of mercy. Scripture reminds us that God is the one who binds up the brokenhearted (Psalm 147:3). Restoration isn't about going back; it's about being reimagined in Christ.

Restore doesn't ignore the damage. It honors it. It's the Spirit's gentle work of weaving beauty from brokenness, strength from surrender and purpose from pain. You may not feel whole yet, but wholeness is already being stitched into your story.

## Scripture Reference

*He restores my soul.*
**Psalm 23:3 (ESV)**

## Micro-Practice

Name one area of your life that feels frayed. Invite God to begin mending it.

## Daily Decision

Choose to believe that restoration is possible; even if you can't yet see it.

# Today's Thoughts

# Comfort
## THE FRIEND WHO REASSURES

❖❖❖

## When Comfort Shows Up

Comfort doesn't speak loudly; it listens deeply. When comfort shows up, it reminds you that reassurance is healing.

## Devotional Reflection

In seasons of grief, anxiety, or transition, comfort is often more powerful than advice. Scripture describes God as "the Father of compassion and the God of all comfort" (2 Corinthians 1:3). Comfort is not a solution; it is a sanctuary.

This companion shows up in the friend who doesn't rush

your story, the prayer that meets you in silence, the Spirit who groans on your behalf. Comfort doesn't erase pain; it dignifies it. And when you receive comfort, you begin to remember: you are not alone, and you are not forgotten.

## Scripture Reference
*Blessed are those who mourn,*
*for they shall be comforted.*
**Matthew 5:4 ESV**

## Micro-Practice
Let yourself be comforted today through prayer, presence, or quiet rest.

## Daily Decision
Reach out to someone who offers comfort. Let them in.

# Today's Thoughts

# *Beloved*
## THE REMINDER OF WORTH

✦✦✦

## When Beloved Shows Up

Beloved doesn't ask for credentials. It arrives with truth: You are loved. When Beloved shows up, it reminds you that your identity is secure in Christ.

## Devotional Reflection

In seasons of shame, comparison, or identity crisis, Beloved speaks the gospel's core message. You are chosen, holy, and dearly loved (Colossians 3:12). You are not defined by your productivity, your past, or your pain. You are defined by grace.

Beloved is the voice that silences striving. It's the Spirit's reminder that you are not tolerated; you are treasured. When you welcome Beloved, you begin to live from love, not for it. And that changes everything.

## Scripture Reference

*See what great love the Father has lavished on us, that we should be called children of God.*
**1 John 3:1 NIV**

## Micro-Practice

Speak this aloud: I am beloved of God. Let it settle into your soul.

## Daily Decision

Choose to receive love today without earning it, without resisting it.

# Today's Thoughts

# *Anchor*
## THE KEEPER OF STABILITY

✦◆✦

## When Anchor Shows Up

Anchor doesn't resist the storm; it holds through it. When anchor shows up, it reminds you that you're tethered to something deeper than circumstance.

## Devotional Reflection

Life's uncertainties—whether relational, vocational, emotional or spiritual—can leave us feeling adrift. Anchor is the companion who steadies us in truth. Hebrews 6:19 calls hope an anchor for the firm and secure. This isn't blind optimism; it's rooted trust.

Anchor shows up in Scripture, in community, in the Spirit's quiet reassurance. It doesn't prevent the waves; it keeps you from losing yourself in them. When you welcome Anchor, you begin to trust that God is holding you, even when everything else shifts.

## Scripture Reference

*We have this hope as an anchor for the soul, firm and secure.*
**Hebrews 6:19 NIV**

## Micro-Practice

Identify one truth that anchors you today. Speak it aloud.

## Daily Decision

Return to a spiritual practice that grounds you.

# Today's Thoughts

_____

_____

_____

_____

_____

_____

_____

_____

_____

_____

_____

_____

_____

_____

_____

_____

_____

# Resilience
## THE SACRED BEND

✦✦✦

## When Resilience Shows Up

Resilience doesn't deny the pressure; it bends with it. There is a saying, "Blessed are the flexible, for they shall not be bent out of shape." When resilience shows up, it reminds you that flexibility is strength and survival is sacred.

## Devotional Reflection

Resilience is not about never falling; it's about rising again, rooted in grace. Scripture says, "Though the righteous fall seven times, they rise up again (Proverbs 24:16). Resilience is the Spirit's quiet work of helping you bend without breaking.

This companion shows up in the moment

you choose forgiveness, in the breath you take before reacting, in the decision to keep showing up. Resilience doesn't mean you're unaffected; it means you're still becoming. And that is holy.

## Scripture Reference

*We are hard pressed on every side, but not crushed, perplexed but not in despair, persecuted but not forsaken, cast down, but not destroyed.*
**2 Corinthians 4:8-9 NIV**

## Micro-Practice

Reflect on one moment you bent but didn't break. Thank God for it.

## Daily Decision

Choose to respond with grace today, even when it's hard.

# Today's Thoughts

# Widsom
## THE VOICE THAT GUIDES

✦✦

## When Wisdom Shows Up

Wisdom doesn't shout; it whispers. It doesn't rush decisions; it invites discernment. When Wisdom shows up, it reminds you that God's guidance is often quiet but always faithful.

## Devotional Reflection

In seasons of uncertainty, Wisdom is the companion who helps you pause, pray and perceive. Scripture tells us, "If any of you lacks wisdom, let him ask of God (James 1:5). Wisdom isn't just knowledge; it's Spirit-led insight that helps you navigate complexity with grace.

Wisdom shows up in counsel, in Scripture, in the still small voice that nudges you toward peace. It doesn't always give answers; it gives clarity. And when you welcome Wisdom, you begin to trust that God is not just present; He's guiding.

## Scripture Reference

*Trust in the Lord with all your heart; lean not to your own understanding; in all thy ways acknowledge him and He shall direct your path.*
**Proverbs 3:5-6 NIV**

## Micro-Practice

Ask God for wisdom in one area of your life today. Listen without rushing.

## Daily Decision

Choose to wait before reacting and let discernment lead.

# Today's Thoughts

_____

_____

_____

_____

_____

_____

_____

_____

_____

_____

_____

_____

_____

_____

_____

_____

_____

# Courage
## THE STRENGTH TO STAND

✦✦✦

## When Courage Shows Up

Courage doesn't erase fear; it walks through it. When courage shows up, it reminds you that faith is not the absence of fear, but the decision to trust anyway.

## Devotional Reflection

Courage is the companion who stands beside you when the path is hard. Whether you're facing conflict, change, or vulnerability, Courage says, "You are not alone." Scripture reminds us, "Be strong and courageous for the Lord your God goes with you." (Deuteronomy 31:6)

Courage doesn't mean you feel brave; it means you choose to act anyway. It's the Spirit's strength rising in your weakness, the quiet resolve to keep showing up. When you welcome Courage, you begin to live not by fear, but by faith. Courage tells fear to be quiet and step back. You may be in the room, but you won't own the conversation.

## Scripture Reference

*Be strong and courageous. Do not be afraid for the Lord your God goes with you.*
**Deuteronomy 31:6 NIV**

## Micro-Practice

Name one fear today. Invite God's presence into it.

## Daily Decision

Take one step that fear has tried to block.

# Today's Thoughts

# *Provision*
## The Faithful Giver

✦✦✦

## When Provision Shows Up

Provision doesn't always come in abundance; it comes in sufficiency. When Provision shows up, it reminds you that God sees your need and is already at work.

## Devotional Reflection

Provision is the companion who meets you in lack—not always with excess, but always with enough. Whether you're facing financial strain, emotional depletion, or spiritual dryness, Provision says, "God will supply." Philippians 4:19 assures us, "My God will supply all your needs..."

Provision shows up in daily bread, in unexpected kindness, in the peace that passes all understanding. It's not just about resources; it's about trust. When you welcome Provision, you begin to live from gratitude, not from lack.

## Scripture Reference
*And my God shall supply all your needs according to the riches of his glory in Christ Jesus.*
**Philippians 4:19 NIV**

## Micro-Practice
Thank God for one way He's provided today no matter how small.

## Daily Decision
Choose to trust God with one unmet need.

# Today's Thoughts

# *Forgiveness*
## THE CLEAN SWEEP

✦✦✦

## When Forgiveness Shows Up

Forgiveness doesn't deny the wound; it releases the weight. When forgiveness shows up, it reminds you that freedom is found in grace.

## Devotional Reflection

Forgiveness is the companion who helps you let go—not because the hurt didn't matter, but because healing matters more. Whether you're holding guilt, resentment, or regret, Forgiveness says, "You are free." Scripture reminds us, "Forgive as the Lord forgave you" (Colossians 3:13).

Forgiveness doesn't erase the past; it transforms it. It's the Spirit's work of cleansing, restoring, and releasing. When you welcome Forgiveness, you begin to walk lighter, love deeper, and live freer. Forgiveness assists you in releasing the weight that is pulling under the waves of life and causing you to drown while the person that you forgive has been and is swimming freely through the waters of life. In other words, forgiveness is for you.

## Scripture Reference
*For if you forgive men their trespasses, your heavenly Father will forgive you.*
**Matthew 6:14 KJV**

## Micro-Practice
Say aloud: "I release this to God." Let grace do the rest.

## Daily Decision
Choose to forgive or ask for forgiveness today.

# Today's Thoughts

# *Purpose*
## THE TREAD THAT HOLDS

✦✦

## When Purpose Shows Up

Purpose doesn't always come with clarity; it comes with calling. When Purpose shows up, it reminds you that your life is part of something sacred.

## Devotional Reflection

Purpose is the companion who helps you see beyond the moment. Whether you're in transition, recovery, or uncertainty, Purpose says, "You are here for a reason." Scripture affirms, "We are God's workmanship, created in Christ Jesus to do good works" (Ephesians 2:10).

Purpose doesn't require perfection; it requires presence. It's the Spirit's invitation to live intentionally, even in small things. When you welcome Purpose, you begin to trust that your life is not random; it's redeemed.

## Scripture Reference
*We are God's handiwork, created in Christ Jesus to do good works.*
**Ephesians 2:10 NIV**

## Micro-Practice
Ask God, "What is mine to do today?" Listen with openness.

## Daily Decision
Do one thing today with sacred intention.

# Today's Thoughts

_____

_____

_____

_____

_____

_____

_____

_____

_____

_____

_____

_____

_____

_____

_____

_____

_____

_____

_____

# Presence
## THE GOD WHO STAYS

✦✦✦

## When Presence Shows Up

Presence doesn't always change the situation, but it changes the atmosphere. When presence shows up, it reminds you that God is with you, even here.

## Devotional Reflection

Presence is the companion who doesn't need words. In the quiet, in the chaos, in the ache, Presence says, "I am with you." Scripture promises, "Never will I leave you; never will I forsake you" (Hebrews 13:5).

God's presence is not earned; it's given. It's the Spirit's nearness in prayer, in worship, in stillness. When you welcome Presence, you begin to live not just for God, but with Him. And that changes everything.

## Scripture Reference

*The Lord your God is with you,*
*the Mighty Warrior who saves.*
**Zephaniah 3:17 NIV**

## Micro-Practice

Sit in silence for two minutes today. Whisper, "You are here."

## Daily Decision

Invite God into one moment you would normally face alone.

# Today's Thoughts

# Closing Blessing

May our God meet you in every companion;
In brokenness, with mercy;
In hope, with promise;
In Peace, with Presence.

May Grace go before you,
And courage rise within you.
May you be anchored in truth,
Rooted in love,
And resilient in spirit.

May you walk not alone,
But with Christ beside you;
The one who restores, redeems and remains.

You are held.
You are known.
You are beloved.
Amen.

# The Root Room

*A place to go and tend to what's feeding your rise.*

# SACRED SOIL

_____

_____

_____

_____

_____

_____

_____

_____

_____

_____

_____

_____

_____

_____

_____

_____

# Sacred Soil

_____

_____

_____

_____

_____

_____

_____

_____

_____

_____

_____

_____

_____

_____

_____

_____

_____

_____

_____

# SACRED SOIL

_____

_____

_____

_____

_____

_____

_____

_____

_____

_____

_____

_____

_____

_____

_____

_____

_____

# SACRED SOIL

_____

_____

_____

_____

_____

_____

_____

_____

_____

_____

_____

_____

_____

_____

_____

_____

_____

_____

_____

_____

_____

# SACRED SOIL

_____

_____

_____

_____

_____

_____

_____

_____

_____

_____

_____

_____

_____

_____

_____

_____

_____

_____

# SACRED SOIL

_____

_____

_____

_____

_____

_____

_____

_____

_____

_____

_____

_____

_____

_____

_____

_____

_____

_____

# SACRED SOIL

_____

_____

_____

_____

_____

_____

_____

_____

_____

_____

_____

_____

_____

_____

_____

_____

_____

_____

# Sacred soil

_____

_____

_____

_____

_____

_____

_____

_____

_____

_____

_____

_____

_____

_____

_____

_____

_____

_____

_____

# SACRED SOIL

_____

_____

_____

_____

_____

_____

_____

_____

_____

_____

_____

_____

_____

_____

_____

_____

_____

_____

# SACRED SOIL

_____

_____

_____

_____

_____

_____

_____

_____

_____

_____

_____

_____

_____

_____

_____

_____

_____

_____

_____

_____

_____

# SACRED SOIL

_____

_____

_____

_____

_____

_____

_____

_____

_____

_____

_____

_____

_____

_____

_____

_____

_____

# Sacred soil

_____

_____

_____

_____

_____

_____

_____

_____

_____

_____

_____

_____

_____

_____

_____

_____

_____

_____

_____

_____

_____

_____

www.ingramcontent.com/pod-product-compliance
Lightning Source LLC
Chambersburg PA
CBHW060413050426
42449CB00009B/1962